# THE ABC's OF A BADASS BITCH

FOR ANY KICKASS WOMAN
WHO WANTS IT ALL

## COURTNEY ANIXTER

To those with a realist's mind and a dreamer's heart

ISBN: 978-1-54396-951-1

# Acknowledgments

## (If I must ...)

It is no coincidence that this book came at a time when I needed to be inspired and empowered. It's hard to be positive, driven, and lead a full life. I'm a doer by nature, and I don't sit on the sidelines. You get one shot at this life and you better make it a damn good one!

Thank you to all of the badass women out there who are making shit happen for themselves, following their dreams, and harnessing a take-no-prisoners attitude. Your energy is contagious!

Thank you to my ever-supportive friends (including my patient male besties). My girlfriends—you are my soul sistas of choice and I am so lucky to have your guidance, honesty, and love. Sweet you rock and sweet you roll, ladies!

Thank you to my editors at Manufixed—Sam and Cristina. You've been with me every step of the way of my writing career, providing sound advice and constructive criticism. Both necessary to my growth as a writer and an individual.

Thank you to my exceptional PR team. Leslie and Julie are quite the dynamic duo and the epitome of women supporting women.

Thank you to my therapist for teaching me the importance of loving yourself, practicing self-care, and accepting acceptance. (Hardest pill to swallow as an adult. *Yuck!*)

Thank you to "my people"—manicurist, trainer, colorist, parking garage attendant at my gym, etc. ... basically those who I see more often than some of my friends. As a collective, you objectively listen to my horrible dating experiences, make me feel beautiful, and help put air in my tires. For a single gal, you're invaluable.

Thank you to my parents for allowing me to pursue my passions in life. It's an incredible gift and one I most definitely don't take for granted. (Sorry, Mom, I apologize for my occasional profanity. I'm still a lady.)

Thank you to my three older brothers. You taught me to be tough, strong-willed, and not to take shit from anyone (even you). Haha.

Thank you to my extended family for being part of this journey with me. Knowing you have people in your corner rooting for you makes anyone feel like Rocky—*"Yo, Adrian! I did it!"*

And, finally, thank you to my five special nephews and, of course, their mothers for giving me my favorite title: Aunt Courtney. (Hopefully, this book secures my "cool aunt" status.) Boys—your mountain is waiting! *Oh, the Places You'll Go!*

# Introduction

This is for you.

YOU—meaning EVERY FREAKING BADASS BITCH ON THE PLANET!

If you're single, you're awesome!
If you're married, kudos to you!
If you're undecided, amazing!

This book's got you covered.

Consider this your pocketbook reference when you need a quick
reminder of your incredible talent, spirit, and soul.

You've got this, girl!
Don't let anyone steal your glow.

And we all shine on ...

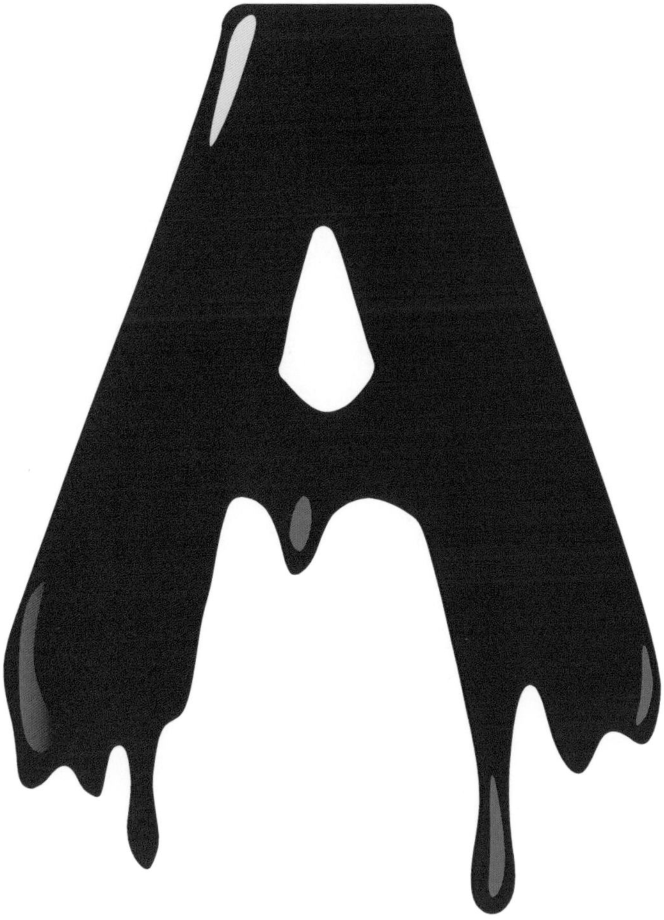
A

# AmBITCHon

## That's right! Get it, girl! It's not 1950!

Women do a lot more than clean the house, fix dinner for the family, and wait for their husband to get home from work. (If you're content and fulfilled doing that, then by all means.) My point is women today have options and should take full advantage of them. For starters, I never dreamed of driving a minivan. No way. No how. Not even my mother was, for lack of a better word, "domestic." (Love the lady dearly, but she didn't know her stove was broken for two years. Case in point.) I definitely ain't being cooped up all day in the kitchen. It's a big world out there full of things do, explore, and people to see! Your internal dialogue is your biggest obstacle. If you think you can, you will. If you tell yourself you can't, guess what, you won't. Don't listen to what society says you should be doing. Do what makes you happy. Adopt an attitude that works for you and stick to it.

Be you!
That's what gives you an edge.
Never lose your edge.

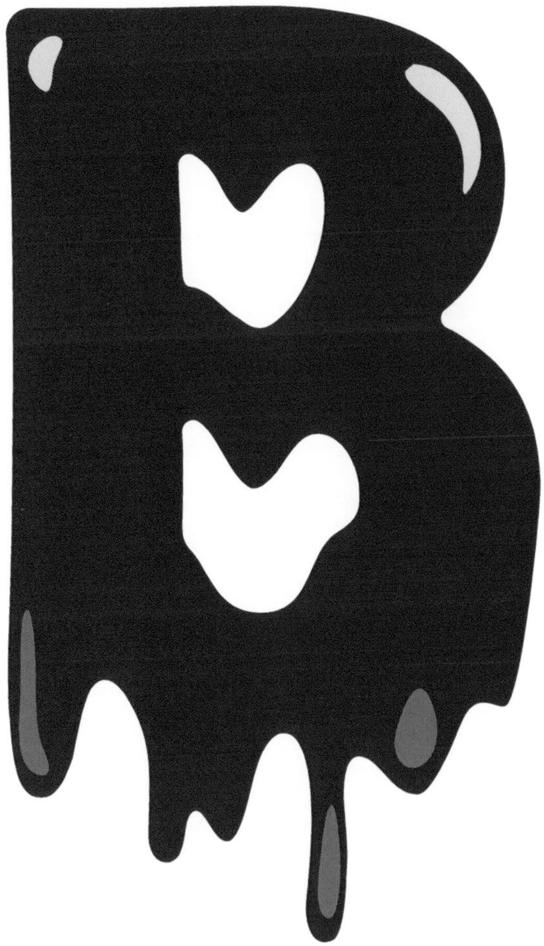
B

# Badass Bitch

*Duh.* You're a fucking monster. You slay.

Being a Badass Bitch means not giving an F. Don't take this in the crude "I don't give a fuck about anyone or anything" way. I'm simply saying that we should discard ideals and labels that make us believe we're total failures in life. *I'm too fat. I hate my thighs. I'm old AF. I'm still single. I'm not pretty enough or smart enough.* IT'S ENOUGH!!!

YOU ARE ENOUGH! REPEAT THAT TO YOURSELF!

Let go of everything that bothers you and set it free. It's incredibly healing. Badassery is a state of mind. You're an unstoppable force of nature. An intoxicating goddess. If someone makes you feel less than good enough, F them! Besides, most things people say have more to do with them and their story than they do with you. Hopefully, you're not a self-centered narcissist, but something tells me this book wouldn't have made its way to you if you lacked complete and utter self-awareness.

Give yourself a pat on the back right now.
You're totally winning.

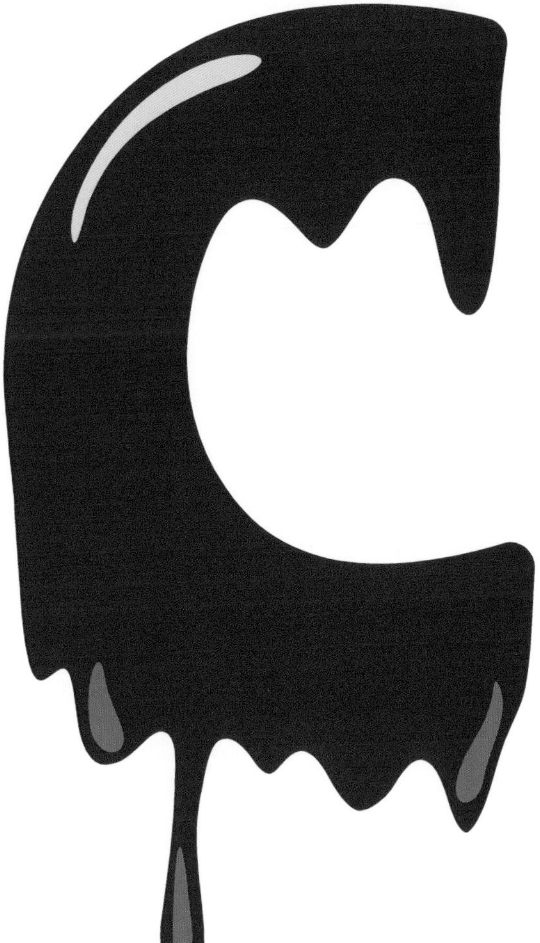
C

# Carbs

They're so fucking good! Right?!?! The struggle is real!

I love bread. I love garlic bread. I love pizza dough. I love bread when it's fresh out of the
oven. I love bread dipped in olive oil. And don't even get me started on pasta.
*Mamma Mia*, here I go again ... I tend to carbo-load like I'm running a marathon.
Fine, cauliflower anything is a nice, nourishing substitute. (Insert obligatory pause.)
Fuck it, it's not the real thing and we all know it. It's a vegetable. It's not supposed to be freshly baked dough.
Same goes for zucchini noodles. Spiraled or spaghetti'd, it's still not pasta! So eat the fucking piece of bread
or swirl those noodles around your fork! If you have celiac or a gluten allergy, my condolences. Carbs,
Chinese food, and chocolate chip cookies are my three C's of kryptonite. I cannot resist, and a Badass Bitch
shouldn't have to! Don't feel guilty about eating. It's a dangerous vicious cycle and one girls know all too well.
Instead, choose to have a healthy relationship with food.

Don't deprive yourself of deliciousness.
Indulge every once in a while; you'll live.

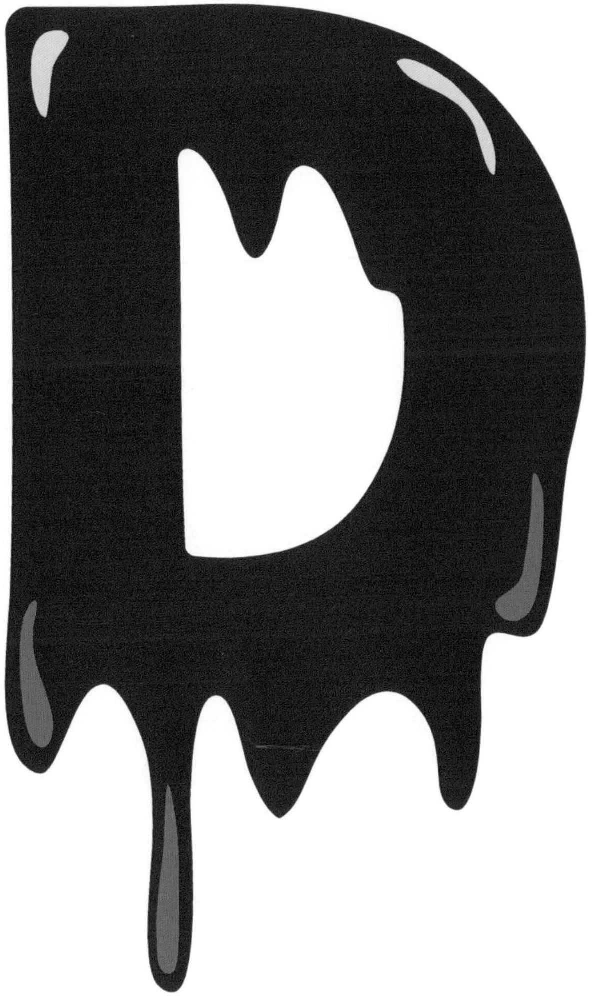
D

# Douchebags

Your twenties are for douchebags.
Your thirties are for weeding them out.

Dispose any unwanted trash and word to the wise—don't recycle unworthy men. You're doing nothing for the environment. They suck and absorb way too much energy. Sure, Mr. Big was sexy and devilishly irresistible, but he treated Carrie like crap. (*Gasp!* I know, it pains my sixteen-year-old self to admit, but it's true. He was an asshole and emotionally unavailable. Horrible combination for a healthy relationship.) Release yourself and break free. You cannot save him. He doesn't need to be rescued. He's not some project. Don't lie to yourself. He won't change and that will be the same sob story you will tell yourself years later. Do not waste precious time. Those diabolical Peter Pans will never grow up because they don't have to. They will find other women who enable their immature bullshit. Don't be one of them.

You don't want to spend your life babysitting an overgrown frat boy.
It's not a good look.

P.S. If he still aspires to get shitfaced and go tailgating with his buddies every weekend—
*"Houston, we have a problem!"*

Ditch the keg and find yourself a real man.

# E

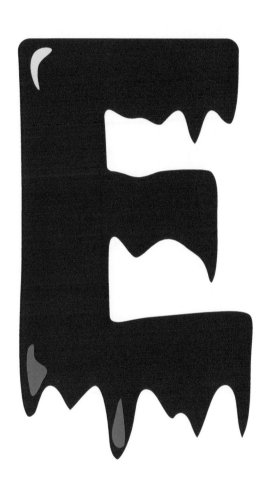

# Equality

*Who runs the world? Girls!*

I cannot stand anyone who thinks women are beneath them. If anything, we are superior. We rule all. It's about fucking time women get paid the same as men. It's still a problem everywhere. How is this even possible? You shouldn't need a man to do anything. That's a really powerful statement. And my future husband will know—I love him because I chose him, not because I need him. Independence is salvation and sexy as hell. Walk tall, girlfriend! Be relentless in your pursuits and partnerships. Furthermore, it's a joke that people think they have the right to tell us what to do with our bodies. In the words of Rachel Green, "No uterus, no opinion." Literally, without our vaginas, you wouldn't exist. Our bodies are vessels for human life. We're pretty fucking sick. And the men who hate women—are you fucking serious with that bullshit?

Don't ever let anyone make you feel less than extraordinary.
You are a masterpiece.
You're a Warhol surrounded by a bunch of wannabes.

# F

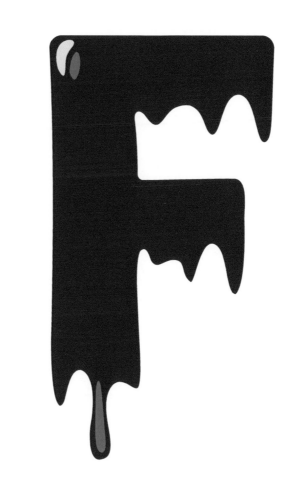

# Friends

"Could this *be* any more obvious?"

Both the TV show and in real life.
Never forget about your friends.

They are your family of choice. Sometimes you get it right when you're five and find your original crew. Other times you encounter truly sublime people as you walk through this crazy life. Carry each of them along. They all serve a special purpose. Every single person you meet is for a reason. Some stay, some leave, and some last forever. Seize every opportunity to tell your friends how much they mean to you. Write a card, send a text, or pick up the phone and call them once in a while. Busy is the lamest excuse. I don't care if you landed Ryan Gosling's doppelganger, don't drop your friends ever for anyone. Because if by chance he dumps you, then you will be screwed and only have *The Notebook* to console you.

*Friends*, the TV show, taught us that real friendships last a lifetime if you nurture them and honor each other. And you never know, your best friend might be the love of your life you never saw coming.

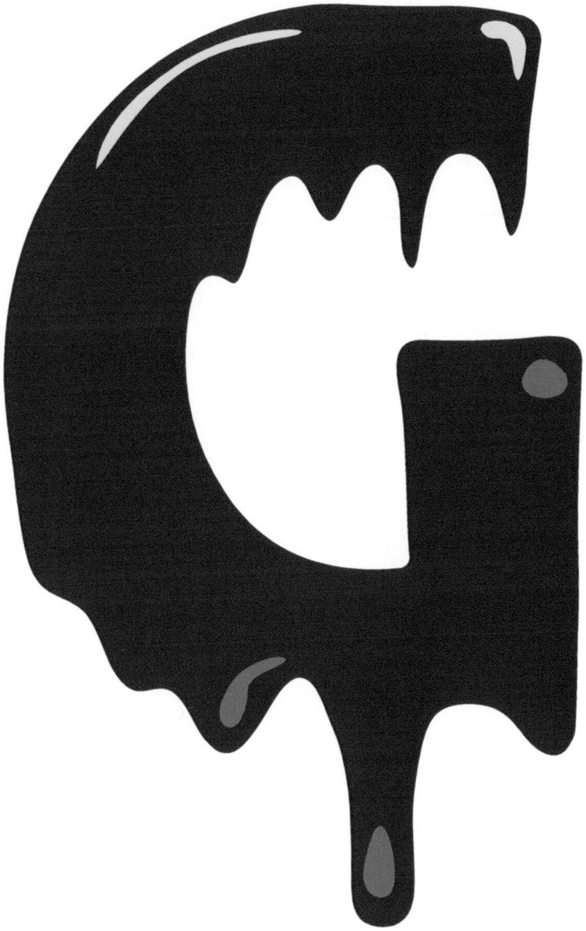
G

# Gucci

## Gucci's made a comeback and so can you!

You don't need designer to feel desired, but it's certainly rewarding to save up for that bag you've been dying for. You deserve it! Fashion and labels can be tricky. If there's anything we learned from Phyllis Nefler circa *Troop Beverly Hills*, "Too many accessories clutter an outfit." Less is more. In the '80s, my mom's college roommate rocked a white t-shirt tucked into jeans with a Hermès belt. I thought she was just about the coolest thing to ever grace my existence. That same outfit is still en vogue today because classics never go out of style. Be confident and daring in your choices. Be anything, but basic. Don't always conform to the norm. It's okay to stand out from the crowd and make a little noise. You don't always have to blend in. And if Gucci isn't your bag, find something that speaks to you and treat yourself. Create a unique brand and flair. Subscribe to your own vibe.

And, finally, always invest in yourself—you're your most valuable asset!

# H

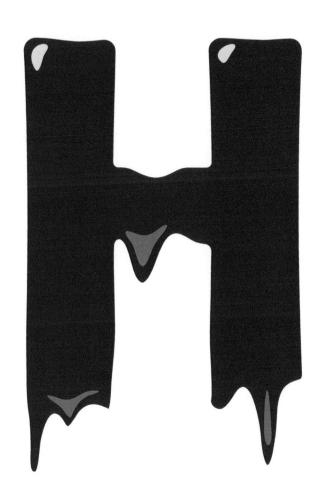

# Hustle

## Set goals for yourself.

Put in that effort everyday to wake up and be the best version of YOU! It takes passion, grit, and an awful lot of self-talk. With no-chip polish, there is literally zero excuse why you can't bust your butt to achieve every single thing you want. Sprinkle some sparkle in your nail game, chop your hair, or go wild with new highlights! Change it up! You'll instantly feel refreshed! Show the world what you're made of! Push yourself, even when it's hard—especially when it's hard. Get out there! Go on! Sweetheart, if the Chicago Cubs can win a World Series, anything is possible! Don't be scared of what might happen; be more afraid of what might *not* happen if you don't take the leap. "What ifs" are foolish traps leading to wicked head games involving only one player—you.

Fearless is fierce.

Being bold requires us to be a little bit brave.

You have to learn to stand on your own two feet and if you want them
to be in Manolos, then, girl, you better work for it!

# Instagram

## Get the FUCK off your phone!

Heads up, literally, so you don't walk into a pole! Social media is an absolute shitshow, not to mention a platform for people to showcase their highlight reels. Don't buy into what everyone is trying to sell you. It's all one big façade. A charade of filtered lives and uneventful milestones. Who gives a fuck what your friend storied last night? Or Chrissy Teigen for that matter? (Sure, she's super fun and outspoken, but you can miss an update about breastfeeding for one day.) And I don't post my food. I eat my food. I don't even have time to get a good picture because I am too busy shoveling it all in my mouth. (In case it wasn't obvious, please reread letter "C" for Carbs.) Don't seek validation through likes from people you barely know. You were amazing before the post and you're still amazing after the post.

(Even if Rise made you look like Chrissy Teigen.)

Stop scrolling and start living.
Set your phone down and be present.
#tbt it for later or never.
Live your life offline.

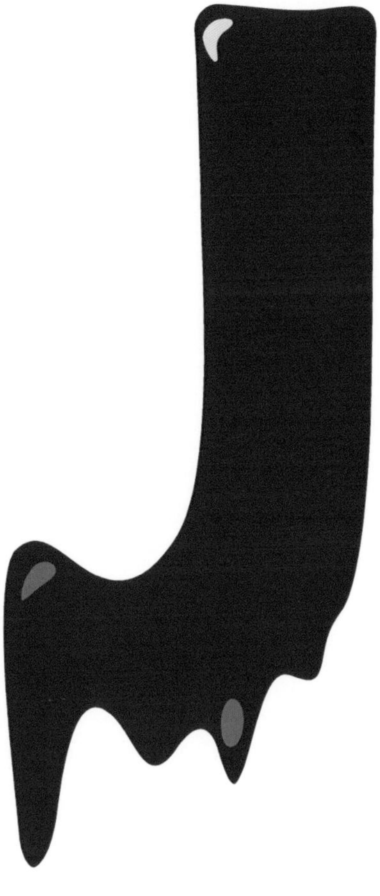
J

# Jagger

PUMP UP THE JAMS!
(Like you're at a Bulls game in the '90s.)
Let's get this party started!

Never stop listening to music. Throw on your Stones tee and start rocking out solo in your very own apartment. Music fuels my soul and my life. There's nothing better than live music on a summer night. *Just Like Heaven—show me, show me.* Be Penny Lane and gather all of your beloved Band-Aids to see your favorite group play, even if you're stuck in nosebleed seats. You won't regret it! Music is universal and also the best cure for anything—heartbreak especially. *Hello?* Nobody does a breakup ballad better than Adele. Just "Shake It Off" with some TSwift if you're feeling twenty-two. Bring your sexy back with the Southern gent of style—JT. And don't forget our female anthem from Ms. Keys because, girl, you're on fire—*OH, OH, OH!* Relive high school and roll down your windows streaming Dave Matthews Band's *Crash* album. Nostalgia is one of the greatest gifts music brings.

It reminds us of moments we quickly forget.

Recapture your moments in life and crash into them all over again.

# K

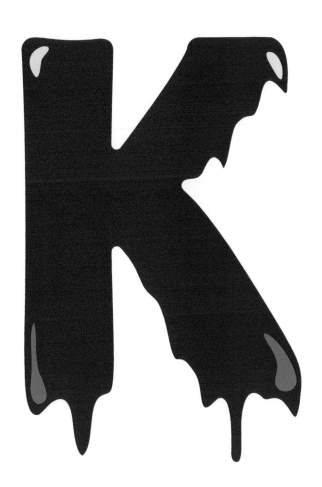

# Kardashian

## Turn off that shit right now.

They are a waste of your time and energy. Don't keep up with them. I stopped recording after Scott Disick, a.k.a., "Let the Lord Be with You" (I mean, I can't), punched a hole through a wall. There was another "K" family dynasty reigning in town before them anyways. First stop, Hyannis Port. The only thing I would pay attention to is how the Kardashians built their empire. They have millions of followers on all of their social media platforms; Kylie was on the cover of *Forbes*; Kendall apparently can be selective about her modeling gigs; and, well, we all know how Kim started. But they fucking worked for it and now they are enjoying their fancy cars and closets full of designer crap they probably got for free. I'm not a hater and I celebrate anyone who hustled to get where they are, but instead of spending your time watching them, make your own moves. They're on the cover of *Us Weekly* every other week, so if you miss something, you're sure to find it there.

Create a name for yourself even if it doesn't begin with the letter "K."

L

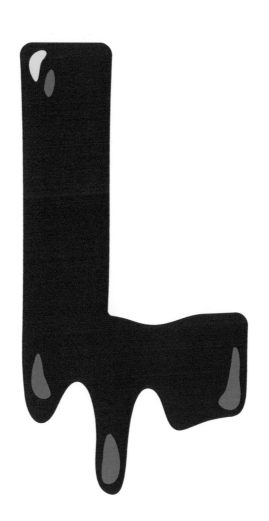

# Level with Me

Are you still here?

Did I lose you already?

Have you moved on to checking your ex's Instagram stories?

Reread the letter "I" one more time, in case I didn't make myself clear.
He married her and he can also see you stalking him.
She sucks. It sucks.
We get it and we've all been there!
It's okay if you looked.
I'll forgive you.

Now back to being a Badass Bitch!

# L

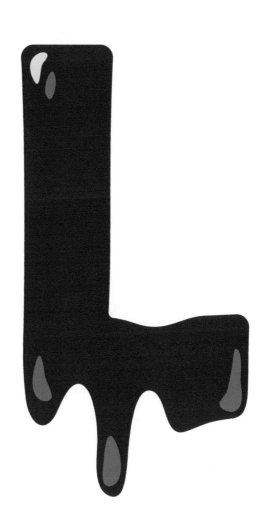

# Love

Yes, I can have two L's.
Badass Bitches make up their own rules, kid.

Love yourself so much it hurts. Drench yourself with your love.

You radiate. You shine. You matter. Love every part of you, even the blemishes only you can see. Love yourself enough to wait for the right person. DO NOT fucking settle. Life is messy and complicated and it will be even more so if you have to live or "make do" with someone who you can't stand. (Any divorced person will tell you that and they do!) Love someone for the right reasons. Love your life because you only get one. Love every single moment you have on this planet and do something meaningful with your time. Love your family. Love your friends. Love the people in your life who make it wonderful. Love your favorite sweatshirt that sits in your closet year after year because you can't bring yourself to purge. Even when you don't want to, always choose love. You'll fare better.

And do not lie to the people you love.
Be honest and be real.
We love you for it.

# M

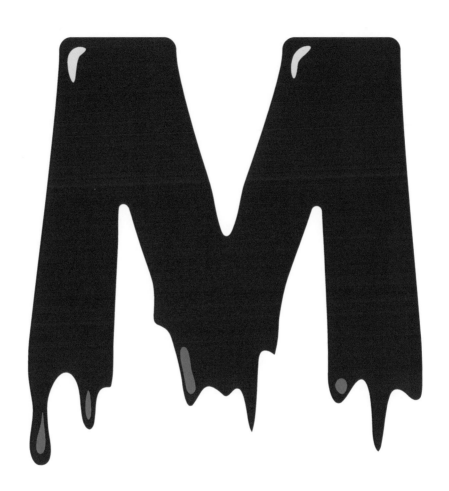

# Mom

My mother will be shocked I gave her a letter.
We tend to butt heads on occasion.
She was Team Jolie and I was Team Aniston.
Need I explain more?

But sorry, Mom, this isn't actually about you. I've wanted to be a mom my whole life. Okay, so I let my Tamagotchi die in the closet because I didn't feed it. *Big whoop!* It's excruciatingly painful to reach a certain age and not have the one thing you've desired. To all the women out there who want to be a mom, I feel you. I'm giving you an enormous hug right now. And to all the women who are moms, bravo! It's not an easy job! And to all the women who decided not to have children, I hear you too. You can be a mother in other ways besides raising kids. Mothers come in all shapes and sizes and whatever you decide is best for you, I stand by your choice and you should too!

Let's be mothers together and lift each other up and say, "Everything will be okay."
Because it will be and we should continue to support each other no matter what.
That's really representing a community of women.

# N

# NO

## Learn how to say "No!"
## It's empowering.

Stop dragging your ass to parties you don't want to be at. Exercise your right to free will. If you don't wish to go somewhere, Nancy Reagan that shit and "Just Say No!" Remain true to yourself and your decisions. If attending a child's birthday bash is going to make you feel horrible about yourself and where you are in life, then just send a gift. Your friend, if she's a real friend, will understand. (Besides, those indoor trampoline places smell atrocious. *Barf!* I wouldn't subject anyone to that, let alone my friends.) If you don't feel like eating dinner with people who aren't your vibe, then politely pass. It's not being rude or selfish. It's self-care. There's a difference. You don't and shouldn't justify yourself to anyone. *"Sorry, I can't make it."* Done. Buh-bye. *Thank U, Next*! Yes, some occasions are obligatory. Such is life. I get that, but if it's not, then bow out gracefully.

Stand up for yourself and only hang where you feel loved, supported, and valued.
Anything less is not worth it.

# One & Only

## Let's officially be done with this concept of "The One!"

You can have more than one. In fact, we deserve more than one; we deserve multiple, if you catch my drift, Meg Ryan! Thanks a lot, Disney and *Pretty Woman*, for making us believe we aren't whole on our own until we found that one person to complete us. YOU COMPLETE YOURSELF, *Jerry Maguire*! It's Cinder-fuckin'-rella bullshit washed down with contrived Nancy Meyers (whom I admire dearly) storylines and designer homes. Besides, how can you find "The One" if you don't even know who you are? Learn about yourself and what you want out of life and then add another person into the equation. *The whole is equal to the sum of its parts.* (Whoa, a dose of high school math thrown your way!) Don't succumb to outside pressure or this idea of a "soulmate" being your be-all and end-all. Times have changed! And this age-old fairytale business only sets you up for disaster. I'm not down with love or a quitter and I will meet the person meant for me, but on my terms.

Bottom-line: A Badass Bitch writes her own stories.

*And she lived happily ever after ...*

THE END

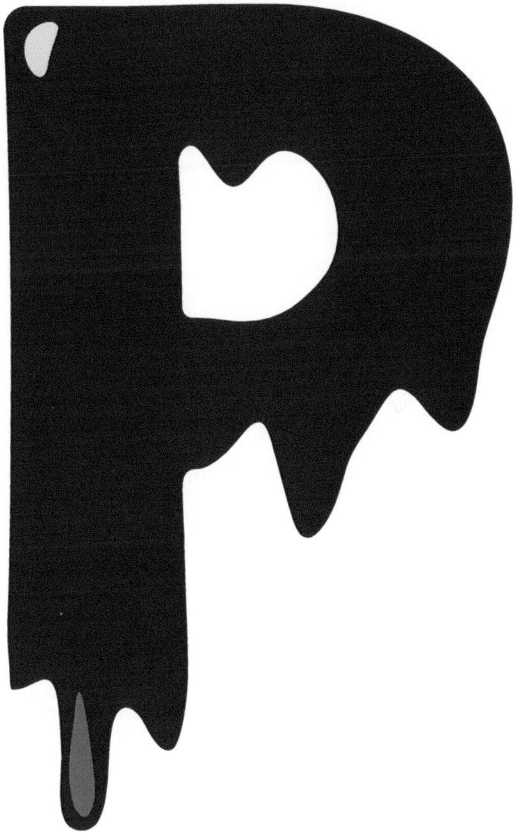
P

# Pity Party Perspective

In the words of Michelle Tanner, "Oh, Please!"

Of course, I throw myself pity parties because life is hard for everyone for different reasons. It just is. It's your party and you can cry if you want to. Take that time to feel every wave of emotion. If you're sad, be sad. If you're anxious, be anxious. Let it all marinate. It's okay to not be okay. Close your eyes and give yourself a timeout. And then wake the fuck up; Badass Bitches don't sulk and wallow for very long. Recognize everything you do have. If you have a roof over your head, food on the table, and people in your life you can count on, you're plenty rich. It's all about perspective and if you need a dose of it, get involved, volunteer, and give back. Surround yourself with likeminded folks who "get it" and comprehend the meaning of gratitude. You won't even need to explain yourself. It's the most calming feeling in the world when someone just gets you. If you ever feel alone, stop and look around at how full your life is.

Open your eyes—BADASS BITCHES ARE EVERYWHERE!

# Quest

## Binge is the new bulge.

If you're wondering why a muffin top suddenly appeared over your jeans or your gym membership expired, one word: Netflix. It's addicting and a bottomless pit for someone with limited self-control. SHUT IT DOWN! A Badass Bitch doesn't sit around watching other people's stories; she writes her own. (Yes, repeating and reiterating my point in letter "O" because it's fucking important! Your life. Your story.) Get off your ass and go on a quest for actual fun. Make big, extraordinary plans. Constantly be curious. The best way to evolve is through experience. Tap your inner adrenaline junkie for a day and skydive or go night sledding down a mountain. (Disclaimer: I am not responsible for any unforeseen accidents. And I only did that when I was twenty and out of the country.) Embrace a different culture. Taste unique foods. Take a road trip! Plan an exotic vacation. Switch up your routine. You need to simply sit and watch the waves crash sometimes, but not all the time.

Be someone who says yes to spontaneity and always have an updated passport!

#wheelsupbitches.

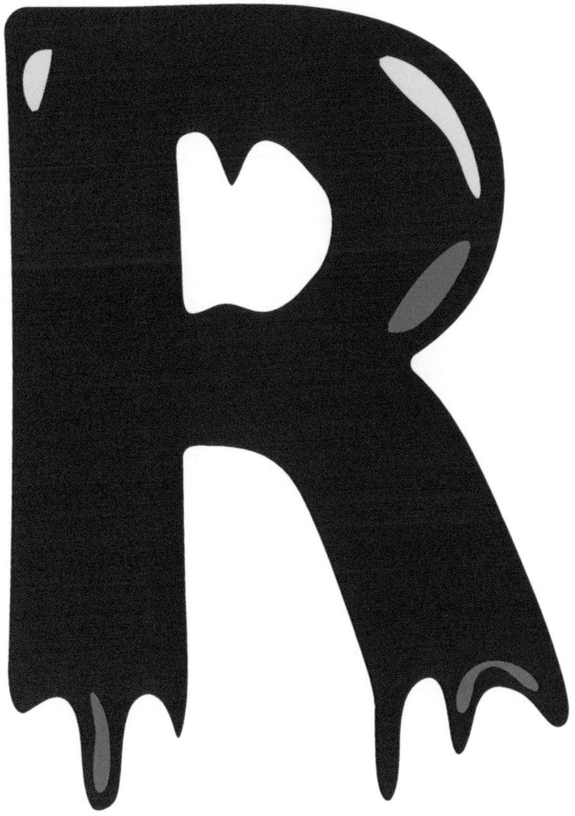
R

# Rodman

Do you remember the basketball player Dennis Rodman?
(Notorious "Bad Boy" and neon hair ring a bell?)

Well, they called him "The Worm" because he always found his way to get the ball and rebound every shot. FYI, you're gonna face setbacks. It's inevitable. You might be a tank, but you're not invincible. There will be days where you don't want to get out of bed, so stay in it, but when you do find the strength, peel yourself out. Breakups are crushing, especially when you thought you met the person you were going to spend your life with and instead there's an unexpected third-act twist. *(Duh, I'm still mourning Brad and Jen.)* You've got to roll with the punches and get back up. Be the fighter they never saw coming. "Eye of the Tiger," Rocky or Rodman! Weasel your way through even if it's tough to crawl forward and force yourself out there. Rodman was an original Badass with a rebel heart. Unlock your secret Badassery (if you haven't already ... we are on "R" here ...) and let the world see.

You're stronger than you believe and a world champion in life.

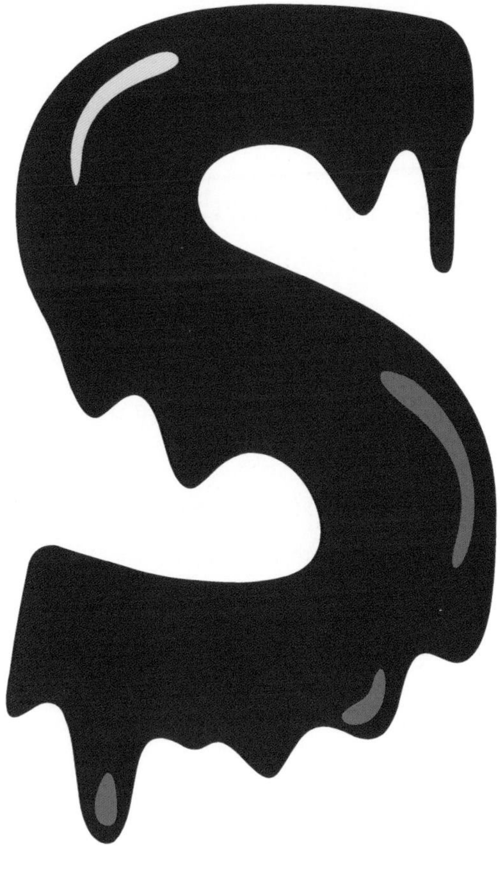
S

# Superhero

## Yep, you've got to be your own superhero.

Don't worry you can choose a fancy cape! Seriously, did you think superheroes were just for kids? *As if!* There's a reason comic books and Marvel movies continue to have remakes, sequels, and different chapters. We need reminders that ordinary people can do extraordinary things. And guess what? You're one of them! Obviously, you're a fucking warrior! You have to learn to save yourself because nobody else is going to do it for you. It's not easy. But it's certainly possible, not to mention necessary. You have all the resources, you just need to use them properly and toward your advantage. And here's the fabulous part—you get to channel your creative side. Yes, you have one even if you're totally left-brained. Would you ever think to call Lady Gaga, "Stefani Joanne Angelina Germanotta"? Or Tina Fey, "Elizabeth Stamatina Fey"? And who the F is Alecia Moore? Calm down, it's Pink!

Be Sasha Fierce and invent an alter ego.
Who will you be and what's your secret superpower?
Ready, set, go!

# T

# Therapy

## Work on yourself.

It will be the hardest work you ever do, but also the most rewarding. (Yep, more work. *Gag!*) Newsflash—your parents aren't perfect. And the minute your rose-colored glasses come off is when you'll really start seeing. If you don't deal with the stuff in your childhood, it will manifest its way into adulthood whether you realize it or not. Accountability is one of the cornerstones of growth. Without it we're just adult children crying for our bottles and pacis. You need to learn how to use your emotional tools in order to overcome obstacles in life. Think of your favorite toy as a child. If you threw it on the ground and it shattered everywhere, would it be the same? Probably not, but you would find some way to put it back together. That's really what therapy is—pulling yourself apart only to bring yourself back together while at the same time discovering the pieces that make our lives whole.

Adulting is draining, but essential.

Badasses tackle their problems, even the tricky personal ones.

#sorrynotsorry.

# U

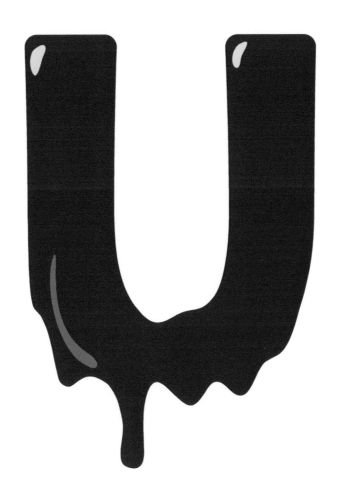

# Universe

Trust the shit out of it. It knows what it's doing.

I wasn't an original believer, but I'm a total convert. Mind you, there will be moments when you lose faith and wonder why you can't catch a break. Stomp your feet if you must but remain focused and resolute. Make lists, envision your life, and pray to the universe. Corny? Yes. But it will hear you. Listen to the messages it's sending back and then act on your instincts. It's more powerful than you and it's important to believe in something bigger than yourself. Imagine there is some mystical force creating magic for us to implement on our own. Wicked cool! A rabbit can't pull itself out of a hat. You have to put in some of the work too. Be courageous enough to fight for your future. Manifest your own freaking destiny! You have to believe with your entire heart that you deserve everything you want and it will eventually find its way.

Trust the process and yourself!

# V

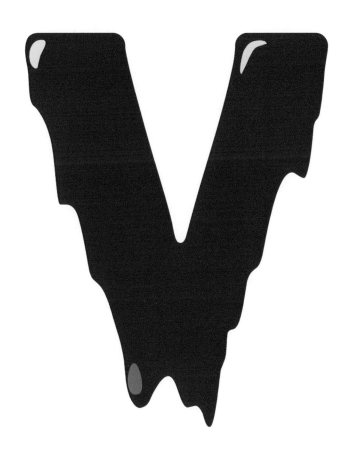

# Vehicle

### Be in the driver's seat of your own life. Don't be a passenger.

Live your life for yourself and make no apologies. You will never be happy if you are living your life for someone else. Stop pleasing everyone. It's exhausting and a surefire way to wind up miserable. Stick to your lane. Leave those negative noises in your rearview mirror and coast. Lock the doors and fasten your seatbelt because life is one exhilarating adventure, if you're ready for it! I hate to burst your bubble, but even with Google Maps or Waze, you're bound to veer off course. That's totally fine. Detours are merely gateways to fun. In fact, you'll discover getting slightly lost is often the best bit of the trip. The unknown is extremely uncomfortable, but it's also really exciting and unpredictable. Sit in that discomfort for a little and listen to music, the latest podcast, or call a friend during traffic. Be one with the open road. It's your bitch!

You'll finally understand people when they say, "Life's a journey, not a destination."

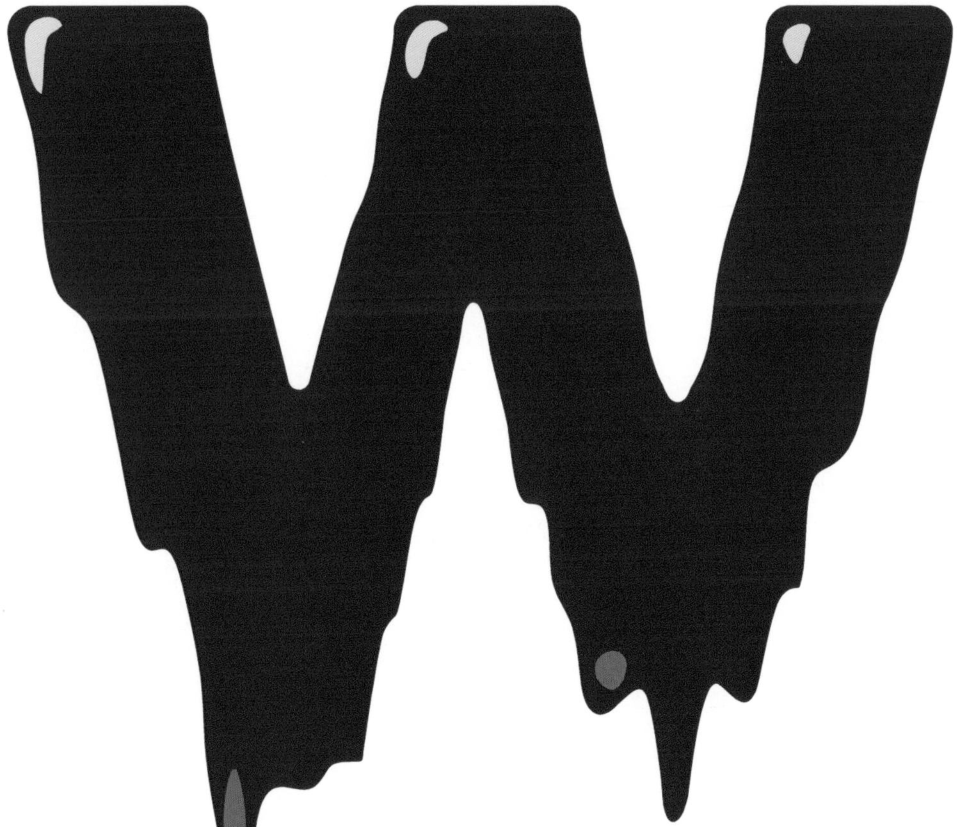
W

# Worth

### Learn your worth. I cannot stress this enough!

If you know your worth, you can walk away from anyone who doesn't. And you should! It's the most empowering thing you will do for yourself. You will not tolerate disrespect at any level from anyone. Set your limit and set limitations for others. Of course people are flawed and imperfect. However, once is a mistake, more than once is a decision. Use your voice and show people you've made a transformative shift. They will notice, believe me. You're worth more than your weight, size, and any other physical feature society deems important. Stop being so damn hard on yourself! Pause for a moment, yes put this book down, and glance in the mirror. Let's be real, hold your phone up for another selfie, skip the fucking filter, and love that reflection! Do you see her? She's gorgeous! Part of being a Badass Bitch is knowing who you are, your value, and recognizing who appreciates what you bring to the table.

Don't serve anyone a piece of you who isn't going to savor the whole pie.

# X

# X-Ray

Stay on top of your health! It doesn't discriminate.

Go to the doctor. Get your blood drawn. Okay, so I can be a tad stubborn and don't always rush to seek proper medical attention. #guilty. However, I take full advantage of these walk-in immediate cares. Best invention ever. Be conscious of signals your body sends you. If it's warning you to slow down, LISTEN! I'm like an 80-year-old with my pill case every morning. Turmeric, magnesium, B-complex, vitamin D, fish oil, allergy meds, and whatever else. Study that shit and energize your body. Also, find time to exercise. *Yuck!* I know, I'm not a Namaste yogi person either. Discover a workout that works for you. You will feel better! Minutes are hours on a treadmill and that skinny bitch who hops on the machine next to you in only her sports bra is annoying AF, but fuck her and keep going. Try a new class, spin on your bike to nowhere, or walk outside. Just find some way to MOVE! You have nothing in this world, if you do not have your health.

Your body is a sanctuary. Take care of it.

# Y

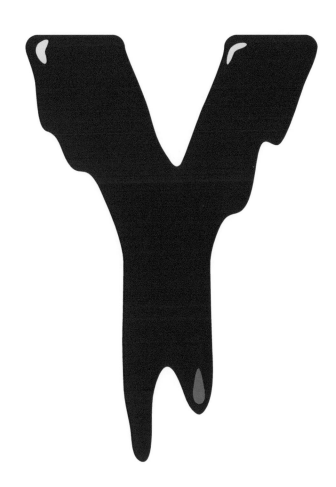

# Youth

Aging isn't for the faint of heart.

It takes real gumption to age gracefully today. Youth isn't just about superficial shit and distinct physical features. We all weren't blessed with Michelle Pfeiffer's cheekbones or Christie Brinkley's genetics. Society seems to want to hold on to everything desperately on the outside, but what about the inside? What about that little girl with hopes, desires, and dreams? Where is she now? Did she get lost? Find her, please! (BTW, she's totally mad you dated a few jerks and starved her for a spring break beach body, but all is forgiven if you honor her wishes.) And if you want Botox to make yourself feel better, fabulous—go for it! I'm terrified of something intended "to remove wrinkles by temporarily paralyzing facial muscles"; however, I do get bad migraines. Quite the conundrum. Wrinkles tell you a story. They show signs of the life you've lived. I love when people smile and reveal their age and laughter lines. It's almost like a virtual time machine. Whatever you do to yourself, do it for you and nobody else.

Love yourself at any number because that's really the trick to staying forever young.

# Z

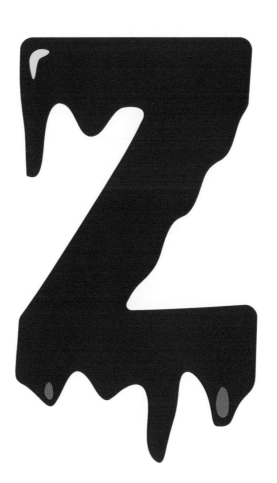

# Zero Fucks

I've said it before and I'll say it again: Give Zero Fucks!
YEAH, ROCK ON, SISTA!

Live your life on your own terms starting now! It feels amazing, right?!? Freedom is sanity mixed with pure jubilation. Cherish this jolt of electricity surging through your body. Sure, we should all still follow the basic common laws of society: treat others how you want to be treated, be kind, blah, blah, blah. You'll do that, but while you're at it be fucking fierce and don't let anyone bring you down. Keep riding this wave of female empowerment and soak up every positive vibe. Dive in folks and scrape the bottom of the ocean! You'll be surprised at what you may find. Spoiler alert: you're that hidden treasure chest of gold. SHINE BRIGHT, WOMAN! And when you do come up for air, choose to be open, authentic, and stop giving a fuck what other people think! Who's with me? (I hope you're shouting "ME!" right now and doing your own happy dance! High five if we ever meet or I'll settle for an emoji.)

#BadassBitchesforlife.

# The End

Keep on rocking in the free world, my friend!
Thanks so much for reading!

(*Duh*, a Badass Bitch always minds her manners!)